The Adventures of Gnarls and Beau

Written by: Mary Beth McSweeney

Introduction:

These are the adventures of Gnarls and Beau – two little dogs with big personalities! Two dogs with different owners who end up becoming roommates also become friends forever, but it was a rough start for the two little dogs...

As for Gnarls, his owner rescued him from a shelter when he was just 2 years old, and she found out that he had been abused before she adopted him. So Gnarls did not like men or other dogs, and he didn't trust anyone except his new mommy, whom he loved and fiercely protected. And because he was always in defensive mode, no one could ever really see how loving he was to his new mommy (always giving her kisses and love); but he loved his new home and his mommy with all his heart. Gnarls was a Chihuahua mixed with Jack Russell terrier, and he was tiny but would growl or bark or even try to bite anyone except his mommy, whom he trusted completely.

About six months later, Gnarls' mommy got a roommate, and she had a dog, too; and his name was Beau. Beau was a small poodle, and he was also a service dog for the disabled; and he was fun-loving and playful, and he loved everyone – even Gnarls, who growled at him for the first two weeks (and Gnarls had to be kept in his cage to keep from attacking Beau or Beau's mommy)... Beau was twice as old as Gnarls, but he still had a lot of puppy dog energy left in him!

Beau immediately loved Gnarls and Gnarls' mommy, but Gnarls was very hesitant to give any love back; however, after a couple of weeks, Gnarls began to see that Beau and his mommy were okay, and Gnarls warmed up to them and was able to come out of his cage to play and share the love.

Chapter 1:

Besides being small dogs, Gnarls and Beau had a lot in common, especially the fact that they both loved their mommies; and they were both big protectors of their moms. Once Gnarls came around to having another dog in the house, he really started to like Beau; but by this point, Gnarls had scared Beau off a bit with all his growling and barking and trying to attack him.

So it took little Beau some time to get used to the new loving Gnarls. But it did not take long at all for both dogs to become great friends, always sniffing at each other and playing, even sharing their toys and food. And both dogs loved both mommies, not just their own mom; and therefore, both dogs were protective of both mommies, too.

They would each bark or let on at any noise to alert their moms of possible trouble; and they would both love on each other's mom as if she were their own. These two doggies were quite a pair, and they complemented each other well. And they both wanted to be with their moms wherever their moms went.

Beau's mom would walk him once or twice a day, and occasionally, Gnarls would go on the walks with them. They were fairly good dogs on their leashes, not giving Beau's mom many problems walking them. But if they were off their leashes and free to roam, you can bet they did what all dogs like to do – chase anything or any animal they saw outside!

Yes, cats, rabbits, squirrels or any other animal were all aspects of these dogs' chasing desires. So it was best to keep them on a leash or in the fenced-in backyard; however, Beau was a sneaky dog who figured out how to slip through the fence and get out. But luckily, he didn't teach Gnarls this trick. And for the record,

Beau always came back to his new home whenever he escaped the fence, so he really was a good dog.

Both dogs loved going for a ride, and it didn't matter where they were going as long as they could have the car windows down and be with their moms. And both dogs loved sitting in their mom's lap, but when it came to time in the car, at least one of them had to stay in the backseat – if not both of them, but they did not mind where they had to sit as long as they could go for a ride.

Chapter 2:

These two little dogs became the best of friends, always playing together or chasing each other around. Oh, and they loved to steal the other one's toy and take off with it just to get a response from the other dog, which usually involved more chasing or playing tug-of-war with the toy!

But the fun and adventures these dogs shared were only just beginning. As they lived together longer, they really became ready for any and all adventures. And both dogs loved a good a time, no matter what they were doing or where they were! So their mommies had a lot to keep up with when it came to watching their dogs...

However, both mommies were proud of their baby dogs and would do anything for them, absolutely anything! And not only did these two dogs know that, but they really seemed to appreciate that, too. To a great extent, almost all dogs understand their owners and show their feelings – yes, dogs do understand you and know how you feel! Dogs are caring animals, which is why they are known as "man's best friend."

Both Gnarls and Beau took care of their disabled moms in every way they could, always giving them love and attention, and they felt whatever their moms felt, too. But they were such playful little creatures that they found themselves in trouble (with their moms) sometimes. These two dogs were "trouble" apart, but they were even more "troublesome" together...

And that's where their adventures come into play. Walks with Beau's mom were always an adventure for these two little dogs as they always found something new to check out or want to chase. They both enjoyed exploring their neighborhood, and the exercise was good for them, too. Exercise helped these dogs since they both had high levels of energy to spend.

But they both got plenty of exercise at home, too. Playing chase around the house and running off with the other one's toys provided lots of exercise. Not only that, but both dogs loved to play fetch, and it didn't matter which toy they were fetching because they ran as fast as they could to get the toy first. So going out into the yard to fetch the paper for their moms was almost like a treat or playtime – big fun!

Chapter 3:

When Gnarls and Beau weren't running circles inside the house, they were chasing each other in the backyard. And of course, whenever a neighbor would walk by, they would bark to let their moms know; but that never stopped playtime for long. And as all dogs do, they liked to "mark" (pee on) their territory in the yard; and each one of them would try to cover up the other's "marking" to try to claim the yard as if it was their own.

Gnarls and Beau would usually stay by their mom's side, but when it was playtime, it was all about play... Their moms didn't have to supervise them in the backyard so much as they had to in the front yard, which wasn't fenced-in. The front yard was like free roaming for these dogs, and they each had to be watched so that they didn't run into the street or off into another yard.

While these two loved a good adventure, they would still always listen to their moms and do as told – they really were good dogs, just having lots of energy made them somewhat "troublesome". Being off the leash without a fence was like free-reign for these two little dogs; and to them, it meant anything was possible!

Birds, squirrels, rabbits and cats were so much fun for them to chase, but their tiny little legs couldn't keep up with the other animals. They would just take off and chase the animals as long as their little legs would let them or until they just ran out of energy altogether. And when a chase was involved, listening to their moms was out of the question! They were focused on getting to their "prize", focused only on the chase...

The fun these dogs had together was endless, and chasing was just a small part of it.

Chapter 4:

Taking the dogs to the park was a big adventure, because these dogs were always ready to play. And since Gnarls had made such good friends with Beau, he was no longer afraid to be around other dogs, which made things slightly easier for Gnarls' mom. But the park was always a fun time for the dogs, because again, it was like freedom to them!

Whenever they went to a park with a lake, it meant swimming time for them because neither one was afraid to get into the water; however, their little legs wouldn't let them swim too far out and they quickly came back to shore. And Frisbees and balls were extremely fun to chase at the park where there was so much room to run and play.

When it came time to eat, each dog did things differently. Beau liked to be hand-fed by his mom. And Gnarls was a scavenger as he would eat anything, especially Beau's leftovers – he loved to clean Beau's dish for him. And Beau didn't seem to mind as long as he ate enough to get full.

Chapter 5:

Both Gnarls and Beau loved to share, whether it meant food, toys or the other one's mommy. They got along tremendously well, but when it was time to play tug-of-war, each dog tried to show off their strength – and this was a fun game for them, which was played quite often.

When it came to backyard playtime, each dog gave the other one a run for his money (or bone or ball in their case). But when they weren't chasing toys, they were racing each other from one end of the fence to the other – just to see who could get there first! Both of them liked to show off, especially when their mommies were there to see who won the race. And each one of them liked to be praised for winning...

Gnarls got Beau into trouble though when it came to being let out in the front yard, even if mommy was just checking the mailbox and coming right back inside. For instance, one day Beau's mom went out to check the mail and took the dogs outside with her; and she figured she didn't need to put their leashes on for such a short trip, but Gnarls and Beau proved her wrong. They each saw a rabbit in the neighbor's yard across the street, and they both took off running to chase the poor little rabbit. Of course, neither of them was able to catch the rabbit, but chasing off like that without coming back when told got them both into trouble with their moms.

Chapter 6:

Like I said, both dogs loved to go for a ride in the car, and it didn't matter where they were going – not even if it meant a trip to the vet for shots or whatever. Of course, a trip to the vet was a little scary for these two – but nobody likes to have to go to the doctor, whether you are a human or a dog. However, both dogs were well behaved at the vet and usually got treats there for being so good; so trips to the vet weren't all that bad.

But pet stores and dog-friendly stores were a few of their favorite places to go, because that meant getting to go inside with mommy! I think these dogs loved shopping as much as their mommies did, especially when they knew the shopping was for them. Of course, they had to be on a leash, but they loved exploring stores and shopping with their moms.

And of course, visiting their grandparents was big fun for the dogs, too. It was a familiar and comfortable place for them to go, and they always felt like the trip was made just for them (even though the trip was usually taken because their moms needed to see their own parents). But every grandparent is loving and kind to their grandchild, whether it be a human or a dog; and these dogs gave that love right back to them!

Gnarls and Beau truly understood what it meant to love and be loved. And they loved the attention, too, regardless of who it was from. But while Beau loved everyone, Gnarls still had his defenses up around most people just because he was scared; and this made Gnarls not as approachable as Beau was. It was one of the few things that made them different from each other.

But love is a powerful and wonderful gift, and both of these dogs knew it and appreciated it. If only the rest of the world felt that way… Sometimes I think dogs know how to love more than people do.

Conclusion:

Even though it took a little while for Gnarls to trust and love Beau and his mommy, Beau taught Gnarls that it was okay to love and that he could be trusted. And from that point going forward, Gnarls was a new dog, and he had Beau, his new best friend, to thank for that.

Gnarls and Beau had many excellent adventures together, and they were best friends for life. Beau taught Gnarls how to love and trust others, and Gnarls taught Beau how to be even more protective of his mom. They learned a lot from each other, and they truly loved each other, as well as each other's mommy.

Every breed or mixed breed of dog is special. But these two little dogs with big minds of their own were a very unique match. Since their mommies were living together, they saw great changes in each of their dogs, changes they were proud of. It was as if their dogs graduated from puppies to highly trained and lovable dogs just like when they graduated from school themselves. But like most parents, they would've been proud of their special dogs anyway.

Gnarls and Beau practically grew up together, each one teaching the other one a good lesson. The most important lesson Gnarls taught Beau was patience; and the most important lesson Beau taught Gnarls was love and trust. And as they grew older together, their adventures didn't stop, but the trouble-making got fewer are farther between.

Yes, their adventures went on for years and years, and it was always something new and fun to do or learn each day. They enjoyed living together and finding new adventures together on a daily basis. And Gnarls and Beau only brought more and more love to the world (and especially to their mommies) as time went on. At least in their case, these dogs were not "man's best friend" as much as they were "a girl's best friend".

The End

www.ingramcontent.com/pod-product-compliance
Lightning Source LLC
Chambersburg PA
CBHW041831280526
45792CB00006B/2051